HOW TO STYLE YOUR LUXURY FASHION ACCESSORIES

ELLE SMITH

Table of Contents

Introduction

By definition, luxury refers to a state of great pleasure or elegance, which usually involves great expense. In terms of luxury fashion accessories, that pleasure originates from the fabric, design, and style of the material made which could be a scarf, glove, etc. These three factors need to be of the highest quality for an accessory to achieve the epithet of luxury. To contrast a luxury accessory from just an ordinary accessory, we would analyze how fabric, design, and style can be a difference.

Fabric

Any accessory produced from artificial fibres like latex, polyester, nylon or spandex can never be categorized as a luxury. For an accessory to be considered as a luxury, it must be made from 100% natural fibres like cashmere, silk, leather, cotton or wool. Nevertheless, these luxury fabrics have their internal chain of fashion command. For instance, the best type of cashmere is pashmina which is obtained from the softest part of the goat's fleece which explains why it is commonly referred to as the best quality. Moreover, leathers can be classified into several classes; for instance, the kidskin leather and sheepskin leather like Nappa are accepted as superior types of the fabric. In addition, Egyptian cotton has a better prestige attached to it when compared with other cotton types.

Design

One thing fabrics such as merino, silk, leather, and linen have in common is that they have been regarded as luxurious and yet, they have not attained luxury acceptability according to fashion trends but instead, on their premium quality and luxurious textures. Their recognition over the years triggered the creation of skills and enterprises that are still operating at peak performance today. Producers of these fabrics obtained expertise and skills over time that allowed the yarn to be converted to the highest quality cloth.

The launch of cashmere mills in Scotland in the 1800s has granted the fabrics manufactured in Scotland a superior cachet as compared to present day cashmere made in China on the basis of the quality and process of its manufacturing. This is also the situation for Egyptian cotton and hand woven pashmina fabrics produced in the Kashmiri territory of India as the techniques have been transferred through families for hundreds of years.

Style

The concluding distinguishing factor of luxury accessories is their style. Despite the fact that a lot of luxury accessories are now massively influenced by fashion vogue and trends, most luxury boutiques and merchants offer accessories based on classic and fashionable styles. Hand-woven Kashmiri shawls were initially promoted and worn by queens and empresses of Europe as early as the 17th century.

Fashion styling is a complete body experience which includes the accessories and outfits we put on. As the saying goes, *"you would be addressed the way you dress"*. Putting on elegant and luxurious stylish outfits boosts our self confidence; which can be compared to body armour.

These three factors mix perfectly to produce extraordinary Luxury Accessories when worn by the owner.

Essential fashion accessories for men

A gentleman's closet is a masterpiece of design and reveals his work ethic. The items in the closet differentiate the real men from the others and for most men, having the proper closet can be a huge problem to handle. It's actually not straightforward, and to some people, it may appear like time wasting. Nevertheless, once you have the suitable accessories together, setting up the right closet is not difficult. Here are items which every man would generally need.

1. **Watch**

Watches are the only luxury hand accessory most guys would love to spend their money on, and it is really helpful; which makes it an extraordinary timepiece. It's a lot better having just one fairly nice piece than disgusting and ugly looking watches. It appears awful when you have a gentleman in a fabulous outfit only to be sabotaged by a terrible looking timepiece.

2. **Tie**

The more the number of ties that a guy has, the better. But then, you need to be mindful of the way you select ties as it is very crucial to avoid cheap ties because they would look substandard even if you wear it with luxurious shirt and suit. Purchase a tie you can afford, but also consider that you need to opt for a stylish material.

3. **Wallet**

A lot of men go for years without getting a replacement of their purses or tidying it. Luxurious and affordable wallets can be purchased without problem in stores.

4. **Money Clip**

Money clips make it easy to carry money around without appearing disorganised. The majority of successful guys understand how they can set up the best public perception by having money around in clips instead of in their wallets.

5. **Messenger Bags**

Messenger bags are a symbol of extravagance and luxury and can be used to keep quite a number of items. Fashionable messenger bags for men match an attractive looking outfit, and the most desirable aspect with men's messenger bags is that they come in different sizes and colour.

6. **Socks**

Even though socks have been a classic part of men's luxury fashion for many years, the art of socks can be a bit complex. However, choosing the ideal socks has never been a problem for some guys. Cotton socks have been the most desired preference of fashion socks for a lot of men and the right colour needs to be worn to blend with the colour of the footwear.

7. **Scarf**

Most guys believe that a scarf can only be used by ladies; however, this is not usually the case. You can purchase a quality scarf and have it on during the winter season to help you stay warm and appear attractive. It can be combined with a pea jacket or an occasional coat.

8. **Belt**

A high quality leather belt, much like an additional simple pair of sneakers can last you for a very long time. Black and Candy Brown are among the colours that can create big distinction if you would like to look special in the crowd. These colours are perfect because they can easily fit properly with all your suits.

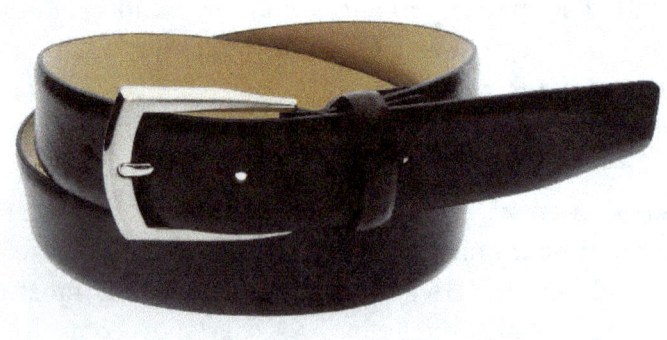

9. **Sunglasses**

Apart from providing protection against sun rays, sunglasses also contribute to a touch of luxury style. There are lots of designs available, and one of the best is the aviator frames. Sports sunglasses do not lend themselves to formal wear.

10. **Cuff Links**

Wearing Cufflinks with your outfit enhances your respectable and professional look. There are numerous smart and neat cufflink designs you can select, and they can be manufactured from different kind of materials.

Essential fashion accessories for women

Although fads and fashion trends transform yearly but one thing that every woman's wardrobe must contain is a combination of luxury accessories she can use repeatedly to enhance any outfit. Accessories can contribute a personal touch and add more design and style to a simple dress.

Certainly, the larger the collection of accessories you have, the more chance you have for blending and complementing styles and creating something totally new. The truth is there are some never ending fashion accessories that you would consistently take out of your wardrobe almost every day for use. Here are ten of those timeless luxury fashion accessories that every woman ought to have in their wardrobe:

1. An extra-large handbag

Teeny weeny clutch handbags are ideal for fancy nights out on the town, but you can't have a lot in them. With a befitting oversized handbag, you can have all you would need in it. Such bags have an additional benefit of making your hips and arms appear tinier too.

2. A statement pendant

The get and go statement necklace will perfect any outfit you are wearing, and it creates the opportunity to express your outlook of style. Dazzling and striking, or more elegant and classy, a statement pendant is the very last minute accessory for an outfit that takes the simple to the extraordinary.

3. Sunglasses

Have a pair of nice sunglasses in your handbag, considering that you can never predict, even in the wintertime, if the sun will shine. They not only cover the eyes from the rays of the sun; they also look fashionable and attractive. If you purchase a quality pair of sunglasses, that compliments the shape of your face, they can make you look as luxurious as any Hollywood celebrity.

4. A black wrap

A basic black wrap is perfect for all formal night occasions. It will keep you warm as you walk from the vehicle to the reception. Wraps should not cover up dresses. The black variant matches with any outfit, and won't have to stand in line in the wardrobe since you could simply fold it into your bag.

5. High-heeled Shoes

Another one of the adaptable luxurious fashion accessories for women is a pair of closed, high heel shoes. These simple favourites go a long way to make any dress look a lot more glitzy. They can be combined with a cocktail outfit, or donned on a pair of jeans. High-heeled shoes perfectly fit with just about any outfit.

6. Black leather gloves

A pair of gloves in the wardrobe is very useful for winter periods. They are basically beneficial to keep the fingers and hands warm, and they prevent a rough and dry-looking skin. You might not need any other pair of gloves if you have a black leather glove set already, simply because the colour black matches with most clothing.

7. A neutral scarf

A grey, brown or black knitted woolen scarf will keep you warm on a breezy winter's day and, however even if fashion trends changes, your neutral scarf would still look fantastic with everything. It's not just for the usefulness of repelling cold at a distance; a neutral scarf always adds a great stylish touch to a winter dress.

8. A pearl necklace

If you would love to splash out some cash on any luxury accessory, then treat yourself to an extremely beautiful pearl necklace. This is a piece of jewellery that will last permanently and will be in style for years to come. You could even have it used by your kids. Whenever you get that pearl necklace out of its container and wear it, it will make you feel like a million dollars.

9. Belts

Do not belittle the effect that an ordinary belt can have on a dress. Belts appear fashionable and attractive, and they bring more clarification to your waistline. Belts (either wide or narrow) add more charisma to an outfit and makes for a flawless fit. If you check around, you will find reversible belts, with a unique colour on both sides, and that will increase your pieces of belts for half the price!

10. Black tights

Black tights can make a dress look slightly official, and they are ideal for both work and night wear. Opaque black tights go well with patterned or plain clothes, and they make the legs appear thinner too. Black tights are well-defined necessity for your luxurious fashion accessories drawer.

Is luxury fashion affordable?

Magazines and TV style spots often tell us how to "get the look" of popular celebrities, but often the alternative style suggestions are still too expensive for most of us. Most of these style sightings exhibit what's currently hot and trending, so is it still worth investing in a £268 outfit based on a multi-thousand dollar one? It may be worth investing in the long term when considering some classic or basics, as most of us can get away with the same looks for less with the help of a little ingenuity.

One of the easiest methods for finding luxurious looks for less is to scour for sales and vouchers. Sales happen all year round, but there are certain months where it's best to buy seasonal items. Even waiting a mere month into a new season can make time for sales. While earlier sales tend to take less off than the end of season sales, they are still worth checking out. If you see some items, you would like for spring when it's still winter, hold off until mid-April, and you'll see items from February and March already on sale. Also, some shops will validate vouchers or store credit given in a previous season, for use during a specified time period. Though most places no longer allow the use of multiple vouchers on a single transaction or do not accept vouchers on top of sales prices, you can still keep them up your sleeve for that special non-marked-down item. Savings are savings, no matter what the discount.

For trendier styles, it may not be worth buying a top-of-the-line product. If you have any interest in styles that are part of fads, buying cheaper clothing may be the way to go. The price is worth the make if a style is not guaranteed to last past the season. You would not want to spend too much on an item that will only end up being hot for a few months? While it is still worth investing in well-made, top-of-the-line classics, such as a nice go-to pair of jeans or a little black dress that will last you years, it doesn't hurt to buy cheaper trendier items that you can mix and match with your wardrobe staples to keep it looking fresh and updated.

What Fashion Accessories Can Do For You

Ladies love updating their appearances, at least when it comes to fashion and style. If you are one of us who have got the zeal for trendy stuff, then you won't be satisfied with just checking out the clothes, since there is an important part that you would never like to ignore -- fashion accessories. Fashion accessories are now gaining more and more attention, though many still do not have a clear idea what exactly they include.

Quite a number of items can appear on the list of fashion accessories, among which you will find belts, handbags, purses, watches, jewellery, shoes and some others. These accessories come in different sizes, shapes, styles and brands. Targeted customers are also under segmentation, with fashion accessories designed for different categories of people, like little children, teenagers, adult men, adult women, the elderly, the thin and the plump, and so on. I have to say that we should give our thanks to the development of the market, which presents to us the innumerable choices.

One of the most indispensable fashion accessories, especially to women, is the jewellery. Necklaces, earrings, rings, bracelets are the important members of the jewellery family, and each of them is trying their best to show their special powers as the small highlights to women. It seems that all materials can go into the manufacture of jewellery, gold, silver, stainless steel, jade, crystals, diamonds, and all other kinds of stones, and even plastics, etc. If you choose the right pieces to wear at the right occasions with the right outfits, they can make great and fantastic differences on you, making you drop dead gorgeous. But surely in return, they also have the power to ruin the whole style if you get it wrong.

Another type of fashion accessory I want to talk about should be handbags, wallets, and purses, which are all the must-have items in daily life. However they are now not carried just for the practical functions, as things to keep people's essentials in place. Instead, they do far more than that. These containers have become the symbols of one's tastes and wealth, and that's why most ladies are dreaming about owning the latest branded designer bags, which cost 'an arm and a leg'.

Shoes are also considered as a type of fashion accessory. When we come to shoes, we can clearly see the inequality between the volume of choices for men and women. Women's shoes are always associated with fashion, with countless options of different styles, designs, and colours, unlike those for men; although this is decided by the instinct driven by women loving acquiring beautiful things and trying to look attractive.

Indeed, using fashion accessories can be a great way to spice your styles and light up your days. With the confidence you gain from these gorgeous accessories, you are going to be a lady with elegance and special fascination, so it's important to learn what accessories can do for you and how to make the best use of them.

How to Achieve a Look of Sheer Luxury with One Simple Accessory

Colours, textures, design, and style - these are important elements of the worlds of fashion and interior design. How these different facets interact produces either a harmonized look of class and style or one in which the elements clash, are at odds with each other and appear cheap and simply messy. Take a primarily traditional home interior and try to jazz it up by adding cheap ornamentation and accessories. The result does not bear mentioning. You need to use only quality items to make it work. The same applies in fashion. Take an inexpensive skirt. Add a pair of high-end *Jimmy Choos* or *Manolos* (*Manolo_Blahnik* is one of the world's most influential footwear designers). The result is the downgrading of the shoes. Yet, if you pair the same shoes with a pair of faded and torn blue jeans, it works.

This may sound confusing and, sometimes, it is. Nobody ever said the laws of fashion and good design always make sense. It is often a case of what "should look good or work well together" may not work, whilst what does not and should not work, actually works – sometimes, incredibly well. At times, a high quality garment or accessory will work and lift up an otherwise banal and inexpensive outfit from the doldrums into the realms of class and opulence; at other times, the intent fails miserably. This is not applicable when it comes to the use of handmade silk scarves and shawls. These fall into a very rare category. The use of a silk scarf or shawl is bound to add a look of sheer opulence to almost anything. There is a proviso, of course. The patterns and colours you select for the prime outfit must match or complement not clash.

The reason why women's silk scarves and shawls work so well with a wide variety of styles may come down to their shape. Another factor is the ability to drape or tie silk scarves and shawls almost anywhere on the body. Silk scarves and shawls can be matched with something of an entirely different texture because the result is something of increased depth and dimension. How you tie or drape the scarf or shawl will determine whether the look you are striving for is formal or casual. The fabric of the unique hand-painted designs of the silk scarf or shawl will always make these luxurious accessories reveal their high quality.

It's hard to believe a silk scarf can transform clothing at both ends of the fashion spectrum. You can match a one-of-a-kind silk scarf with either an evening gown or leggings, toss in ballet pumps and achieve the best effect for either look. It does not matter how much or how little you pay for your leggings, canvas pants or peasant skirt. This amazing silk accessory will raise them up, placing them into an entirely different clothing league adding fashion, class, and elegance to the look. By simply adding a stunning hand painted silk scarf or hand-dyed shawl, it does not matter whether the rest of your clothing is either expensive or even high quality. Single-handedly, these magnificently beautiful accessories can increase both your luxury and wow factor no matter what ensemble you trot out.

Why Women Love Fashion Accessories

Today, our society has developed tenfold, and physical looks are important. Physical looks sadly may determine your standard and class. Modern ladies and young girls are pretty much conscious about their looks, and they know all about the latest fashion trends coming out every year or season. Similarly, like fashion trends, fashion accessories have also been seen as an important thing that women can use to stand out in the crowd. In this modern world, the acquisition of fashion accessories has become a way of life.

You will notice one thing about all fashionable women is that it's not always that their clothes are great, or their clothes look great, but often it's the accessories which are well-punctuated amongst the clothes. We often ignore the accessories and just look at the clothes, but accessories play a very important role in shaping how you look.

Fashion accessories can be explained as those add-ons, which are in line with your clothing, as well as acting as an enchancer to your attraction. It is a 'show-off', of your fashion taste. Now, what really can be termed as fashion accessories? Fashion accessories range widely from and not limited to earrings, bracelets, rings, watches, and scarves.

Now, have you ever thought about why women like accessories so much? Here, in this article, we will list four possible reasons, about why women like accessories so much.

✓ First of all, as we said, that women and girls nowadays want to be pretty much updated with the latest fashion trends. Wearing the right fashion accessories just goes on to prove that you are updated with the latest fashion trends. Fashion accessories are often the signatures of your class and elegance. If you are a fashion lover, you will hate if someone calls you out of fashion. If you are a truly fashionable person, your sense of styling should be in popularity. You should always wear things which are trendy.

✓ Fashion accessories are often 'show-offs' to one's social status. We have often seen that famous celebrities wear or carry fashion accessories made from the leading brands, which are apparently not affordable by the common people. But, today, there are cheaper brands, which make the same type of accessories, which also show a woman's fashion attitude.

Wearing the right accessories with your clothes makes you look complete. Today, the modern generation has embraced fashion accessories like never before, and therefore, you are incomplete without wearing some of them with your glamorous clothes. There are many different occasions to attend, and there are different accessories for them. Not only that but wearing accessories will make you look appealing.

✓ People don't take this up seriously, but fashion accessories actually show your personality. People nowadays like to show their special traits to people; since they want to stand apart from the crowd. They like to show it by what they eat, what they wear, what perfume they apply etc. For instance, your way of wearing a scarf will tell a lot about you. Some may wear it in a traditional method; others may wear it draped around.

To sum it all up, fashion accessories have become a woman's best friend. No one can deny the extra piece of attraction that fashion accessories amplify in a woman's body. *Night Queen* is an e-store for women accessories that is fast gaining prominence among girls and women alike. Visit their website to buy something exciting.

How to create custom piece of fashion jewellery

Creating custom jewellery offers, even more, opportunities because you can choose exactly what kind of jewellery piece you want, the exact style, the shape, the colour, and the theme is all in your control. Buying jewellery as is restricts you because you get what you see, and though that can be elegant and stylish, creating your own allows you even greater freedoms and allows you to make pieces that are even more affordable and fashionable. Custom made jewellery will allow you to make just the right piece that you need to match with your favourite dress or outfit, and will give you ample room for creative liberties.

Many craft stores provide basic tools and bases for jewellery making. So, for instance, you can get plain chains, earring hooks, clasps, and undecorated rings, all simple and basic and usually highly cost efficient. These base pieces will provide the platform for all the creative jewellery making that you can begin to do. Equally, if you are not sure what kind of jewellery you want to make, taking a look through the craft store aisles is a great way to figure out what kind of jewellery you might want.

There are expansive selections of beads, pearls, stones, and other accents that you can use to make jewellery that looks like it was stored bought. For instance, you can buy beads that come in transparent and shiny colours and string them together to make a nice necklace, custom selecting the combination of colours you want and the pattern and size of the various beads. Then, you can make matching earrings and a ring, as well. This will allow you to create an entire set that can reflect and be a perfect match for any dress or outfit that you have. Doing this yourself will guarantee that you spend far less on the entire set than you would if you purchased one like it at the store, and the bonus is that you get to have fun as you make your own jewellery. *Hobbycraft* and *Creative Beadcraft* provide supplies for home jewellery-making.

Now, if you are interested in unique and creative pieces, you can try other pieces with which to make jewellery instead of beads and stones. Beads and stones provide an elegant and sophisticated look, whilst other items will provide your jewellery with a creative and artsy flair. For example, using bottle caps, like the ones that come on old fashioned soda bottles or beer bottles, you can make a necklace that is fashioned with all the caps clustered thick till it forms a chunky necklace. You may take the pieces from a hair band or accessory, as many of them have nice objects like sculpted roses or big jewels and decorations and turn them into fashion costume rings that sparkle and shine in your hand and make an explosive statement.

Finally, jewellery that is made with imitation flowers can also make a lovely and elegant statement, as well. You can take imitation carnations, roses, and daisies and string them together to make a floral necklace that will look lovely with spring dresses or with your beach outfit. Flower rings and bracelets are also nice additions to any jewellery collection.

Ethical and sustainable accessories

Ethical fashion or ethically responsible fashion can be explained as an approach to design, sourcing, and manufacturing of clothing, which is both economically conscious and sustainable. It includes all kinds of wears like dresses, jeans, shoes, tops, jewellery, jacket, shirts, blouses, and other accessories. Due to various factors like child labour, exploitation of the workers, low wages, environmental pollution, and other reasons, ethical fashion brands are becoming highly sought after.

Ethical fashions dresses are comfortable, stylish in casual and formal outfits for men, women, children, and elders. These soft and cozy fabrics are ready to wear and ideally suited for summer. Ethical fashion dresses are available from various brands and designers.

If you are looking to get **female** accessories and clothes, you should consider the following brands:

- **Adili** is a popular online ethical departmental store.
- **All Things Green** has clothing accessories for ladies.
- **Amana** offers women clothes in sustainable fabrics, including organic cotton.
- **Beaumont Organic** offers simple; elegant women wear in organic cotton.
- **Belle and Dean** have variety of organic cotton clothes for babies, women, and children.
- **Boutique-Ethique** offers women wears in sustainable fabrics.
- **Chandni Chowk** also has a variety of fair trade and organic clothing and accessories for women.
- **Conscious Elegance** is an Eco-friendly name in wedding dresses and ballgowns.
- **Ethical Superstore** is a famous name in ethical clothing for men, women and children.

- **Fashion Conscience** offers a wide range of style conscious ethical fashion for women.
- **Feral** has organic cotton T-shirts for men, women, and children to support global cooling.
- **Frank and Faith** offers clothes for women, men, and children made in the UK from sustainable fabrics.
- **Get Ethical** has a wide range of ethical clothing and accessories.
- **Goodone** is an innovative name in recycled clothing for women.
- **Green Apple Active** delivers an organic, vegan, and biodegradable bamboo product line of activewear.
- **HUK** offers organic cotton t-shirts for women, children and babies.
- **Jo Pott** (or Jo Pott Mercer) offers fair trade women wear and interiors.
- **Life clothing** is a famous name in fair trade and organic cotton clothing for women.
- **Makepiece** has a variety of women wear elegantly designed and made in England.
- **Thought Clothing** offers casual clothes for women in hemp, bamboo, and cotton.

If you are looking to get **male** accessories and clothes, you should consider the following brands:

- **Ardalanish** is popular for its woollen products and meats from the Isle of Mull.
- **All Things Green** has clothing accessories for males.
- **Ascension** offers organic T-shirts and jeans.
- **The Hemp Store** is a famous name in clothing accessories for all men in hemp and organic cotton.
- **Thought Clothing** offers casual clothes for men and women in hemp, bamboo, and cotton.

Ethical fashion has revolutionized the concept of clothing and wear by strongly advocating and preserving the nature and its resources. By '**Going Green**', people are enjoying natural and easy summer outfits and wears.

Fashion accessories for occasions

The right accessories can completely transform an outfit. An item which started off as a staple dress can be turned into a jaw-dropping ensemble. A t-shirt and jeans combo could become a hip party outfit. In the world of fashion, accessories are everything. However, knowing how to accessorize is no easy feat. What works for a dinner party will not necessarily work for lunch with the girls. Here are the perfect accessories for every occasion to help you get it right.

Casual Day Wear

A lot of people think it's too over the top, accessorizing during the day. Actually, it's one of the best times to dress up a look. There are some subtle looks you can go for when wearing casual outfits. Just coordinating your belt and bag can do the trick. Perhaps a pastel neck scarf, to add some colour. Minimal jewellery is also another must-have. A classic watch or a few cute rings is all it needs. A white tee and jeans can suddenly become a hot, on-trend outfit. Indeed, an outfit that makes heads turn.

Lunch Dates

This is a step up from your casual day wear, but still somewhere you don't want to be too over the top. You can go a little bit more dramatic with your jewellery if you're on a lunch date. We're talking earrings, necklaces, and bracelets that match. Consider the shoes you're wearing as well. Try to coordinate them with your bag and belt, for a more polished look. Leather wallets are a great accessory for a lunch date. After all, you want to show off your style even when you're paying your half. A calf length skirt with a tee tucked in is a real hot look right now. Make sure you finish it off with a waist belt for the perfect lunch date outfit.

Dinner Parties

It's the perfect excuse to get out that little black dress. However, a Little Black Dress can look dull if you don't accessorize. This is where you can really go to town with the different types of accessories. You want to create a look that no one else will be wearing. Pick three key pieces you want to highlight your style. We recommend one piece of jewellery, your shoes, and your handbag. These three should all match in colour or theme. A silver shoe, bag, and bangle are prime examples. Leave everything else simple. Whatever you do, don't opt for all black everything. It's a dinner party, not a funeral.

Night on the Town

Planning a big night out with all the girls? Less could be more when it comes to accessorizing. Too many of us overcompensate with accessories when you go out to bars and nightclubs. Actually, you could be detracting from the main event. You, of course! A discreet clutch bag and matching shoes could be all you need. If you're planning on wearing jewellery, then try to keep it classy. Big and bold pieces with a cocktail dress will only make you look cheap.

You're now prepared with accessories for every occasion. Revamp your wardrobe with just a few small changes. You'll be surprised at what a difference it can make.

Silk Bolero Scarves

Bolero scarves are a classy and multi-functional scarf/jacket that fits with just about any outfit. Perfect for those chilly autumn evenings where you want to enjoy warmth while making a statement.

Step out in style with these elegant silk bolero scarves! Exquisitely soft to the touch and fantastically fluffy, you will love how this lovely bolero makes you feel. Feel like a superstar every time to slip into this beautiful fashion scarf!

Bolero scarves are a high quality scarf that simply gives you that touch of glam. Simply slip your arms inside and wear like a jacket - you'll love how the soft material hugs the back of your neck and helps keep you snug. You will love how all our great fashion scarves look and feel, and how they compliment your outfits. Bolero scarves are a comfy alternative to regular scarves. Easy to wear and always glamorous. Our boleros are a gorgeous addition to your look. Supremely soft and superbly stylish, you'll be able to enjoy fantastic fashion all year round.

Made of 100% Natural Silk material.

Made with LOVE.

Made with PASSION.

Wear with PRIDE.

Find great collections of available quality silk bolero scarves perfect for you at Inspired By Elle.

Conclusion

You should never underestimate the public impression that a luxury accessory can make on you. There is no doubt that having a luxury accessory on with a matching outfit can be a plus to your overall confidence in the environment.

Your appearance is much more different when you are on top of your accessories. These days, there are many people who disregard this element of styling, which is quite strange.

In this book, I sincerely hope you have gained a thing or two about why you should start using luxury accessories whenever you go out.

Visit our website at www.inspiredbyelle.com to see all our amazing offers. Take that step today.

www.ingramcontent.com/pod-product-compliance
Lightning Source LLC
Chambersburg PA
CBHW070957120626
46546CB00004B/1666